Startling

Startling

Andrea Selch

COCKEYED PRESS
Chapel Hill, North Carolina

Published in 2009 by

COCKEYED PRESS

PO Box 3669
Chapel Hill, NC 27515

www.cockeyedpress.com

ISBN: 978-0-9790623-1-5
LCCN: 2008911865

Designed by Anita Mills
Cover photograph © 2001 Caroline Vaughan

Acknowledgments

With thanks to the magazines where the following poems first appeared:

Asheville Poetry Review: "Calving"

Calyx: "Return to Kitchawan"

The Greensboro Review: "Succory"

Luna: "Nightslip" and "Song for Late Spring"

Oyster Boy Review: "The Ballad of the Bee," "YoU," and all six "Twentieth-Century Valentines"

In addition: "The Lithuanians," "Tearing Down the Morris House on Perth Avenue," and "The Morris Supreme Test," reprinted from *Prairie Schooner*, volume 78, number 1 (spring 2004), by permission of the University of Nebraska Press. Copyright 2004 by the University of Nebraska Press.

For Anita, Paul and Helen

Contents

One

Startling

Nipples

1.
Now they are soft, like brown split peas
too-long soaked

and I have forgotten about them
like I forgot the dog's

until, after her surgery, she rolled over
and there, on her shaved belly,

were the eight pink nubs.
So many mouths to feed!

2.
Now they are hard and larger:
hazelnuts, rosehips, Matchbox headlights.

A camisole is no match for them,
but they would precede me.

In the first trimester,
there is no forgetting them.

At 15 Weeks

Since I cannot feel you yet, you're alive
to my imagination. From the amniotic ocean floor,
I watch you swim. Silently, you practice surface dives
and flips—a thumb-sized Esther Williams,
minus the bathing suit.

We are both waiting
for the music to begin.

First Words for My Son

Soft on the heels of your arrival,
a slow bloodletting, and low
in my abdomen, your pillow shrinks.

Now I can hold your whole uncrumpled self
on my forearm, your head on my palm.

Yet the world seems no less dangerous—
perhaps more—here, let me take the bannister,
study each stair: Let nothing disturb you
nor ruffle a single russet hair.

Startling

8/6/00

At first the world comes in in grainy black and white.
Your eyes don't track, but roll and flutter
and I ache for control.

Alas!—you've come without a knob
for horizontal or vertical hold.

* * *

Not hungry yet, you root by instinct—
and do not trouble yourself to swallow.

8/10/00

Only four days from the womb, you breathe
like an athlete—deep in, long out.

What races will you run?
What might you win?

8/11/00

You sleep, and dream
of what you've already learned:
desire, discomfort, the color red.

All else startles you.

8/21/00

My nipples respond to your cries
with white tears.

I cannot feed you enough!

9/6/00

Your tiny hands are buds.
They blossom, finger by finger.

* * *

Already I miss your beginning,
your mute reception of the world,
those startles of the newborn you no longer are.

9/28/00

Still your hands haven't found each other,
nor your thumb your mouth,

yet your eyes know mine
and how to smile,

which is consolation.

The Four O'clock Deer

Like clockwork every afternoon
they come here: five slender gray ones,
coffee muzzles, white tails twitching.
The two who just two months ago were fawns
dare to nibble at the lawn,
their mothers graze the woods,
the other stands and gazes at me
(or so it appears) in the window.
She nods her head, or bows.

Other days I've played this game,
dipped my head submissive or in greeting,
until she didn't seem afraid.
Today, I must resist her stare:
My infant son is crying.
He is hungry, that is clear.

For beauty, now, I'll take his face in sleep,
for playfulness, his laughing squeals and kicks.

Two

Memory's Algebra

Song for Late Spring

And now as May upon the moist streets
slings her longer afternoons, and nights
upon each hard-buffed car
breathes a chartreuse pollen sand,
                              as once again
the August-baked and winter-deadened dooryard
swells with clover, and the clematis
unfurls its purple blooms,
                              speak kindly,
for the first time, of yourself—
review and recompose those many stories
you always told so glibly,
                              as if with Spring
you'd realized a crucial misconception,
such that now your wasted life
appears a fertile basin,
                              where presently
the fallow fields may all be planted.

Return to Kitchawan

1.
Still that same mysterious floor—
each tile a different, solid brown
and yet the parquet shines unwilled,
reflects the inside of the house
as outside, down the hill, the warm lake
holds each fern and leaf for iris and, for pupil,
ponders the clouded August sky.

At three, this house was huge to me—
all closets and stairwells, cupboards
and costume drawers. Outside, the trees
and lawn stretched endlessly and the hill
was dangerous for acorns, but anyhow I ran it
on my still-unsteady legs, headlong
toward the soft part of the lawn, the shore,
and my cousins hard into another
of their sweetly secret games. I guess
I must have said, please let me play,
and one said you're too small, or
wait another year, and I did.

Behind me, in that memory,
the grownups, on the patio since lunch, saw
only the first steps of my descent, turning
at the first of my murmurs of glee,
then turning back to the circle of empty
adult conversation, and I
went down beyond the pointed caps
of acorns, barefoot and alone.

2.
Summers passed—it seemed forever
and one day I came down that hill
and the other children said "follow,

follow"—my one girl cousin led the way,
running here, a skip there, a hop—you know
the game. And, when the rain began, the game
played into the house—I did the best
I could at keeping up, the hill was steep
for me. Up we filed to the attic—
there were bats, or worse, they said,
but I was fearless—following.

That year under the eaves we built
the Black Cat Tavern—gambling casino and house
of pleasure—throwing craps on the sawhorse table,
spinning miniature roulette, then scoring,
first with poker chips and then a sock
or shoe (a single point) or shorts (for their
two legs counting two), cards held high
and close—no peeking. But one rule
I didn't learn from winless games was not to play
as I lay clammy on the mattress ticking
and they examined me, a finger here, a pencil
there—not every child has played that game,
not every girl remembers how her lips
were parted, how—instead of her—
her brother, cousin, spoke: "Look, look."

3.
I shut my eyes, as outside, down
the hill, the wind let out its breath
and blew, blurring the ferns, the leaves,
the blinding greenness all around the lake,
until inside, every tingling nerve had fired and
my brownish summer legs were still.

And memory's erased the pain
of acorns, but the thrill, the fear, that first,
headlong course to freedom, is with me still,
and now, their children down below them,
my cousins argue on the patio
which tree was third base, which tree home.

Self-Portrait at 31: As Persephone

1.

Only now can I see it—who I might have been:
a little girl like the little girl in the etching
I had in my room as a child—tiny smooth body,
a head way too large, and a cat on my shoulder scratching
to get down or get a better hold;
                                        But, at 6 p.m.,
my mother, home a moment for a nap
and then to change for dinner, called me to her bedside
to split a pomegranate, showed me how to free
the red seeds from the white and bitter flesh,
told me to swallow even the pit (to spit
she didn't say would be unladylike—
I knew);
                As I furrowed
the impossible fruit, night fell,
my mother rose and dressed, adhered her lashes,
bound her wrists and fingers with heirloom
golden pieces;
                        Outside, it was almost winter,
and across the back courtyard I could see the kitchens
and bathrooms of hundreds of neighbors
whom I didn't know then I'd meet much later,
when I'd aged forward, become
the woman destiny intended.
                                Persephone,
now, I'm called and, though I can lead you
through the underworld, I yet resist the title,
wondering if there isn't still another path I don't know,
some tunnel that one who came before me chose
and, mistaken, I'll lean after her,
drawn into further darkness, sadness,
the red-walled cavern somehow and suddenly
become a hall of lamentation, tarnished green
as the copper of old playground fixtures

fastened to the granite bedrock
of my childhood city, or as those tear vials
in their tiny cabinets in my mother's bedroom—
antique, curious, and so fragile.

2.
That winter evening my taste was set:
All my childhood onward
the huge rubies of the pomegranate growled to me
from every autumn, window into the dark world
my mother went out into every night—
the bacchanals where men *and* women
drank and whirled, where up till bedtime
all imagined they were bachelors, free to fall
or follow where they would,
but instead, at some magic hour, unchecked
their coats and hailed their taxis home.

I was too young to go, and so, delirious
with loneliness, I took up mental residence
across the back courtyard, in the tiny, untidy rooms
of the lady my mother called Mrs. Saggy Baggy,
and the man (her husband?) whom I saw undress
and sit awhile each evening, imagining myself
their late-life child, solder for a love gone weak
from too little weeping, so much padding.

Meantime, I went on growing, not easily,
but the way a starving child does, in fits
and starts, and hollowly: Knock on my bones
and I rang. Always, so much wanting.

And when we finally left that house—the backyard neighbors
perishing from sight like dreams in waking—
my body swelled and curved, and I went outside...

3.
In this disguise, my work's to tell all stories,
especially the matter-of-fact; what all
you do not question, what you think is gone,
is mine.
   Except my own past, that is,
which is legend now, but to no purpose,
since it's wrong. Tell me, why
does no one ever recognize my will? Why
is my story always told in passive form,
as if one day I was dancing 'cross a meadow,
picking flowers, then the earth yawned open
and I was taken?
   Even *I* am wont to say
that winter evening, by my mother's bedside,
I was less a human child—curious for new dessert—
than blank, inscribable, my mother
or some other force of myth engraving me.
Even *I* thought I couldn't have chosen,
or wouldn't have, or not in my right mind.

But now I have to think again:
When I matured, the taste that grew in me
was for a sweeter fruit: an older man, unknown—
Hades, call him (it doesn't matter, he's gone now).
I went and found him—*I* stole *him*—walked
him slowly home, his hand on my shoulder,
on my behind, between my legs and,
later, in the dingy living room

I went on choosing.
               And how I loved that first night—
sheer madness!
             exactly what I'd wanted.

And though I bled, and though I ached,
I thought—taking madness over sadness—
at least the madness was a mask, a stunning role
I could and have dropped regularly:
bursting back from lunacy to light—my rightful place,
though only halfway filled by me,
as I'm no perfect little girl,
untaintable, unhungry.

4.
Still, there's no question but for access
to this red and bleeding world, I'd still
give half my days and all nights up late reading
when the first words from the mockingbird are mine;
I'd give up youth again.
             Because now they come
to me, those strangers whom I knew from nights
I stayed awake and stared at them, inventing
lives for each in his or her own cubicle,
apartment, *home*, I suppose you'd say, though
no one in them had meant to end up where they did—
all were victims then of fate, and so refused
to call their houses homes.
           Now,
as I set to place those coming on,
I see the rooms I peeped into as *back rooms*—
of all our selves or rooms, most fragile,

undistinguished—and give each one another look,

now see how sadly they so often come, alone,
and even in pairs, one always tugging
at the other. Look how Mrs. Saggy Baggy—
still colossal though this time lovely—
shakes her head at her undershirted husband, *Come on,*
come on,
         as if it couldn't happen
that they'd go together,
                  each one being
and wanting what the other was or wanted.

And to them I am somehow gifted to make magic
of their mismatches—
              eternity—
                    though
still a child, the same one I've always been—
loosely sketched in, out of proportion.

Nightslip

His fingerprints burn, here, on my shoulders.
Night slips bravely into dawn—the street below
lies lavender-empty, undone; in this light,
in the still house, the velvet torso
of the blouse I wore, a silver shimmer—
so soft it could be almost gone. All evening
through it I felt him touching me—or
wanting to—his fingers too light on my shoulders,
too heavy, now I think I can discern their ten
prints on that shirt, which like a dormant cat
slumps in the lap of the green chair by the window.
Look. So suddenly it's real: one sleeve
slinks around—just like a paw searching first
for a rough pink tongue then a dirty ear.
Is this a dream? This late, my eye has lost
its focus, wanting this single fixture,
simple dose of what home should be like:
the comfort of one cat cleaning its ear,
or another, legs outstretched, all belly fur
and tabby stripes. No. No, this cat is shadow—
fancy—absent all evening, perhaps longer, as I
might have been, but did my part—sweet thing—
in velvet. See, even the dreams
go bad in this house—I am sure of that,
yet always I forget, a week or two
before returning—forget and then
remember him (my father), groping
up the stairs, one hand heavy on the banister,
voice thick at the doorjamb, "Please let
me in," and I do, and crush that precious
flower in my hand: Nightslip, I call it,
lavender and green; no leaves, no petals
have ever, when I looked, remained by morning.

Then it seems there was no flower, only
my palm, a graying map of veins, missteps
I've taken, smuggling a different blossom out.

Alphabet: Verso and Recto

August: apples
in my grandmother's orchard
still weren't ripe, and we knew

           Better than to admit
           how the smooth trunks beckoned
           our bare legs, throwing

Caution to the ground,
cloistering ourselves
among the gnarled branches, and

           Dragonflies, below us,
           hummed from rock to rock
           where we pitched the doomed fruit

Even my baby brother was in on it—
not big enough to climb,
though willing, almost

           Five, he held his shirt out,
           emptied each apple
           caught as if

Gold. But the grownups had said,
If you eat them, you'll get
Green-Apple Two-Step

           Hex or dance? I wanted to know
           but the specifics of those regions
           no one spoke of

Illness, if mentioned, also
sounded sweet, and my cousins,
intent on emptying one entire tree

> Just went on as though nothing
> else was wrong, jumping down
> finally, to run and play at

Keep away—almost antidote enough
that we forgot the sterile room above
the dining porch, where our grandfather

> Lay, dying of a brain tumor. There
> the air weighed heavily on my shoulders
> as my mother steered me to his bedside

Maybe he wanted to smile
but his face was flaccid,
like a melted doll's, and I could

> Not touch him. *You could take his hand*
> my mother said. The waxy limb lay
> outside the cotton-waffle blanket

Oh, if only I played chess! Only
a month ago my older brother sat here,
the board between them, making moves

> *Pretty* my grandfather said, or
> was it *Pity*? I took hold
> with my two smaller hands

Qualms...I'd had them.
But in that instant, when I felt
his pulse quicken

Reason seized me, and I knew
why he'd been moved home,
how our shouts and laughter would

Shrink his tumor, sing back
his wry smile, sly wink.
How else heal a pediatrician?

Tenderness, then, came into my heart—
times he trotted me on his knee to Phoenix,
checked my reflexes with a rubber hammer

Unless I'm wrong, I didn't see my granddad
after that. Some part of me
says: Unconscionable. That autumn a

Vacuum formed at the country house,
the vast lawn brown, the apples dropping
to the scuffed dirt and rotting there

Well, I won't belabor it.
Whatever we take from the past—
for convenience, let's call it

X—is what remains
after the years have performed
their long division, tidied the

Y in the apple tree where I stood
aiming Granny Smiths at
Gregory's blond head

Zig-zagging below, and arranged
my granddad's death for the following
Christmas morning: A zero-sum game.

Three

Euphonics

YoU

Because I spent all night
dancing with you
I said last night's prayers
this afternoon

And then this evening
when you were—who knows—
at your home? and I
was here alone, thinking could this love
be true? I found myself

with folded hands, praying anew:
what should I do? what should I do?
After the one-two one-two
of all night dancing with you,
what else could I do?

Oh you honey dew
come back soon. Who cares
if it's true but while it's new
I'd rather my two hands
were full of you.

The Ballad of the Bee

or, Queen Bee's Lament

Listen my liege, my owner, my alpha-king—

You have known me most to quail and quaver,
(I submit, I am not the pit bull
you bargained for, but quite the opposite:
Only in dreams do I quiver bravely,
queering a bunny or bagging a quail)

now, however, I have a big quarrel.
The bone is this: that bi-ped you've been
biting faces and rubbing bellies with—
boy is she quirky! So queasy and querulous,
and worst of all, what's her beef with the beasts?
She won't eat anything that once breathed,
yet she won't properly greet me:
Instead of standing still so I might sniff her butt
or lick her limbs, I must sit quietly
while she slings a soy-snack in my general direction?

Oh, I should've known, that first night you vacuumed
then banished me to the back room, left my bowl
filled with backwash, as if I'd been bad.
I didn't quibble though, thinking
At least it's not a bath!
But there, I barked too soon:
Now, for our quality time (the questing of the ball)
you have substituted a weekly bath and brushing—
quelle horreur!
Now, instead of calling Queen Bee,
you disparage my dander, admonish, "Be Clean!"

What if once I were to bite quickly
(quite by accident of course) her hand

as yet another beef-free biscuit
was bequeathed to me?
Ah the bloodbath, the bruising!

But quit this belly-aching,
I tell myself. It doesn't befit a bitch;
behave, be loyal to the last.

And so, I bay:
Once upon a time, you called me Queenie
and bantered and babytalked to me,
and we walked quotidianly, and on holidays
I quaffed beef broth from a quality bowl.
Now I am "The Bee," second banana,
on the back burner, *baroness*—
But still unbudging: quiescent
in my basket, next to your queen-size bed.

Good Times and Bad

Are all relationships grab bags,
or just the badly-grounded ones?
My guess—merely the latter, where the bitterness
of long-ago battery guts any bravery,
and makes one guarded as hell.

But you and I, despite
our ghastly backgrounds,
when we bonded, galloped:
You were gallant, gorgeous;
I was brave, blunt—
God, but it was good
that groping our way to bliss,
and even after it, the blushing and giggling,
gone, all the butch bravado.
I was ga-ga for ya baby.

And then, by Gum, something else began—
a basic grasping:
Your baby-blues went goo-goo;
and I both boo-hooed and grew grandiose.
In bed, you took my biting for belligerence
and I, your groans for granted.
By February, I was busy busy busy
and you were bummed.

Now, you battle germs and other bugbears,
which bothers me;
and when I grumble, you grovel;
and then I get even more greedy with my time.

Does it boil down to who's more guilty?
Or that I am bi and grungy and gregarious
while you are gay, bookish and homebound?

I won't begrudge us some discord
but Geez, we've got to be bananas for each other.
We're big girls—let's break up.

Succory

Slow, the green came, weaning
the white bud from its tight swaddle of leaves.
Below, the slim stalk hardened;
each evening, stark against the muggy pane,
its veins drew closer in and spined like bark,
and you moved about the room, oblivious.

Never, in this whole slow flowering,
did the blossoms flaunt their vellum blue, but spread
their moth-wings uncertainly as the first
clean sheets we laid together on my bed,
tentative as we lay that following morning,
the first you didn't have to leave.

And now the flowers blow, their whiteness
quelled, and you and I un-sheaf;
you disavow our home
the way a bough lets go a blighted bud. So,
how is it you held nothing and I hold on,
left, at the sill, with only this slow unfolding?

Four

The Truth About Meat

Calving

March 24, 2000

When spring comes, my father thinks of the calving:
Night after night someone must sleep in the barn,
and when it starts—in March—the nights still aren't
above freezing, and the barn not much warmer.

How many nights was it him, he wonders,
the one in the coveralls waiting to hear
that groaning? Cows are dumb animals—
leave them alone and they'll bungle the calving:

in the pasture in the early morning they'll face
downhill and the calf will get stuck. "Turn around
dammit Addie," he said the one time, on his way
home for breakfast, it started to happen,

and pushed at her sweaty flank, trying
to turn her like a spoke in a wheel,
but her feet stayed planted and she groaned more
and went on sweating and straining.

He reached inside her then, like he'd been taught,
arm slick with his spit then her mucous, and felt
for the calf, its front hooves first like two stones,
then its nose like a rubber eraser, and pulled all he could.

But nothing budged and the cow went on groaning
until, as dusk fell, she died where she stood,
and the calf too, little bundle of sinews
and stony feet. When spring comes, my father thinks

if he had them, he would keep his coveralls on,
and the due cows all day in the barn.

The Lithuanians

Christmas, 1997

Face down in the foyer, she lies, that statue my brother bought
from the son of a painter our grandparents befriended
before the Second World War. In the afternoon sun,
her bronze back—slightly arched—gleams
and her hair—black and thick as licorice—
as usual guards her features.

Today, on the corner of her pedestal, by her outstretched left hand
sits the box of songbooks, their covers bearing
merry blue carolers wearing red scarves in the snow.
As the evening progresses, the statue disappears
beneath coats, furs, capes;
an antique top hat slants on her left hip.

They were married in '26, my grandparents, quietly, in Paris:
Both were doctors, but Ruth
was the daughter of a stockyards baron,
and Harry, the son of Samuel Bokvits, a Lithuanian tailor
renamed Bakwin at Ellis Island in '96;
in aught-nine, when Harry was thirteen
and reading in the synagogue on East Eleventh,
Ruth was learning to ride sidesaddle, her brown velvet dress
perfectly sized. Of course it was Paris
where these two exchanged vows.
And afterwards, raw oysters in their stomachs
and drunk on champagne,
doctor and doctor walked the Champs Elysées
and talked of buying art.

And in the '30s, solvent as Marshall Field,
in their brownstone on the Upper East Side,
they held one supper after another, all the artists they knew
shoveling down roast beef and creamed potatoes,

settling on the sofas as Harry's chamber group played Wagner,
each artist, later, sending on a drawing or sculpture.
Diego Rivera was there, and Calder and finally, Ben Shahn—
a tall man, smudged yet not undignified,
ten years nearer Lithuania, with his eyes on injustice:
Dreyfus, Sacco and Vanzetti, sweatshops and the Depression.
Even so, Harry and he became friends, and soon
two of Shahn's watercolors—the Beach at Fire Island, the Clown
with the red face—hung in the front hall.

The Clown still hangs, in fact,
above the coats piled on the bronze his son made
a half-century later,
but the house is changed now my mother owns it: the walls,
a jumble of paintings and prints,
some she and my father bought in France in the '50s,
after she quit medical school; many more he bought,
filling out his history of Revolutionary music
(soldiers stamping, fifes blaring, drums booming);
and here and there, a lesser work
from Ruth and Harry's collection: Kogan, Rivera, Volti, Derain.
(Gone the Cézannes, Van Goghs, Matisse's Woman in Blue.)

Now, instead of quartets and Grade-A beef,
the table is set with peanut-butter sandwiches, buffet style,
and upstairs, with his wife and little boy,
Jonathan Shahn sings "O Holy Night" while, in the foyer,
his lovely sculpture gulps for air.

1979: Tearing Down the Morris House
on Perth Avenue

Except for two years (when a dozen Dominican nuns,
their convent under construction, resided here),
the house of Nelson Swift Morris has been home
for twenty years to the Viatorian Order of Catholic Priests.
Once a model of modern comfort—
thermopane windows, gas-heated racks for drying clothes,
an intercom and walk-in closets—these last two decades
the oaken floors, devoid of carpets, have been polished
only by the monks' prayerful pacing,
                                        and the bathroom vanity,
a marvel of mirrors and pink-streaked marble,
has not seen an eyebrow tweezer, black bow tie
or plunging neckline.   Yet the house seems made for this:
In the wet bar stands a marble altar and walnut kneeler;
the gown room's been a dormitory; the closets, vestiaries;
and, outside in the greenhouse, where Blanche Morris
nursed her English roses when she was at home,
the Reverend John McKee harvests parsley, oregano and chives
to liven the community kitchen's Wednesday soup.

To Father John, the day seems very long,
but tomorrow the damning letter will come:
"The estate of Blanche Swift Morris (née Bilboa) has been settled.
As there will be no more support forthcoming, the diocese
has elected to destroy the building and develop the land
for low-income housing."   And Father John, though he shouldn't
deny the poor, will miss his crimson satin headboard,
and the late-August dips in the blue kidney-shaped pool.

1929: Pearl "Horse" Tompkins and the Mustang

Big Arm, Montana

No one could tame him, least of all me.
I was the only girl who rode that drive,
the only girl for miles, but like all the young bucks,
I still tried—tied on my ropers
and strode out tall and strong—to hide my fear—
but that horse stared at me no different
from the boys, retreated as I closed in,
my lasso furled, knuckles white beneath
my gloves.
                   It began to rain
and in the rain we stood eye to eye, still
as Indians, until our coats were drenched,
till the boys had left the fence and the ground
between us began to steam.
                                        I put down
my rope, for a moment gave up
thinking and breathed a while. His muzzle
was the pearl gray of a fine hat, new,
in no way scarred. Three fingers above
his nostril his coat went black,
absolutely unreflective, though soaked
with rain.
                   We'd named him Benito—a blessing
this single horse alive alone in winter,
but surnamed Juarez, for the way he held
our gaze, would not be touched or bridled,
rebellion of a kind it seemed to us;
                                        to me,
the simple way things were—one could not
be otherwise and still survive out there
on that gusty plain, the rain so often sudden,
unrelenting.

That's why, when the wrangler
said I must return to camp, get dry and fed,
I stood an hour longer and shivered with the old horse
in the tall corral, our two breaths
mingling in the green Montana dusk.

1924: In the Slaughterhouse

"Use everything but the squeal."—Gustavus Swift

First there is the killing—the stunning blow
in the knocking pen, and then, at the sticking rail,
the bleeding: blood steaming from the strung steer
in the uppermost slaughterhouse hall.

After that his head's removed, and he's dropped
to the floor, where his fore and hind legs go to glue.
Next comes flaying and evisceration:
Rehung, the rump's skinned out, the hide pulled free

from the round and then the back, and what's left
of him is sawed in half and scrubbed with water
and dried and finally inspected.
With its skin removed, a carcass appears

all gristle—gleaming fat hanging
by its hocks from the unlikely trapeze.
The ching and whir of the pumps
between the pickling bins and trying vats,

the forced-air fans and the chomp, chomp, chomp
of the inspector's blue-inked stamp is music here.
And there is some rhythm in it—
"cutter cows" and "canner cows" go one way,

carcass beef gets graded A, double-A
and B, and makes its way to hotels,
restaurants, "the better class" of butchers.
And it's a thing of beauty—that the rendered bits

become fertilizers for the fields that feed
these animals all summer long.

1910: The Morris Supreme Test

"We must not fool ourselves. We cannot afford to guess.
We must *know*."—Nelson Morris, explaining why Morris
and Co. began testing its products.

Each week a different worker's family is invited
to dine in the sleek test kitchen of Morris and Company.
This week they are seven all together—they've brought the baby too—
seated on the benches to greet the numbered platters.

Which dish, the father strains to recognize, features
the Morris Supreme fare, the juiciest meat, freshest eggs,
"the clean and sweet and delicious oleomargarine"?
Today, it seems its Platter Two, the dried beef
(prepared with milk and eggs) that betrays
the standard shape required by "the wonderful machines"
that packed them into vacuum tins—no human
had a hand in those perfect medallions.
And yes, they're tasty, they are "supreme."

Yet, to mother, thinking of all the times she stretched
half a dollar through a week of meals, even Platter One,
its eggs congealing, looks appetizing.
"I wouldn't scoff at it," she says, and to her children:
"Eat up now, clean your plates, eat everything."

Five

Twentieth-Century Valentines

Human Papillomavirus (Genital Warts)

Great were the days when each and
Every act seemed blessed by gods,
Not guaranteed to make you
Ill, not a game of truth and dare
That had you thinking back through
All encounters, wondering which still
Lay dormant in your tissues, or

Worse, was just now waking
And would assert itself in symptoms—
Rashes, abnormal cells, too few
T-cells, its awful offspring already
Settled in the one lover you ever really loved.

Chlamydia

Cautious in all things she has always been;
Hardly aware of how it makes her seem that she
Lists among her daily errands even
"An unexpected kiss" as if exact apportionment of love
Might afford this graying marriage a youthful glow.
Yet no prophylaxis—emotional or otherwise—can
Delay the onset of midlife dalliance:
In theory, infidelity is instinctive.
And now, catching herself about to scratch, she knows it.

Herpes Simplex II

Hundreds of times it's happened,
Even hundreds of thousands—the
Rape of little sisters by their big sisters'
Perfect boyfriends; only you can't
Estimate how many, weeks later, felt the
Sores erupting, their painful itching; and

Statistics, for all their social value, do not
Interest these girls (now, women) who must forever
Mumble the truth in time to each
Potential
Lover—the one I knew and made love to
Erred in this, and now no longer can I call myself
Xenophile—but love each year

That passes without a strange and
Weeping sore. Still sorry, though, for
Overreacting.

Gonorrhea

Good things come in small packages.
Old habits die hard.
Neither a lender nor a borrower be.
Only the good die young.
Reality bites.
Real men don't eat quiche.
Hell hath no fury like a woman scorned.
Even in laughter the heart is sad, and the end of joy is grief:
An ounce of prevention is worth a pound of cure.

Hepatitis B

Half a week he can usually refrain from thinking of her;
Especially if he keeps his mind on the domestic market.
Privately he wishes it would have gone differently
And now he'd have her and the child—a son of course,
Thin and strong and with a tropical verve—
Instead of this princess wife and three obese little girls.
Too late, he thinks, then another West Indian accent turns his head;
It's missing her, he's sure, that sends him
Seeking foreign industry and sugar abroad.

Bastard, his wife calls him, when he comes up positive.

Human Immunodeficiency Virus

However long you do live
I will be with you,
Valentine, sweet valentine.

Six

Cancer in Manhattan

Pastoral

Last Monday the turkey buzzards were relentless
circling the clearing beyond the garage—and I
imagined some huge dead animal, a deer or bear,
swollen, on its side, at the field's edge,

making an odor that I wouldn't be able
to ignore in a few days time, and my neighbors
would call, saying, *Say, why don't you look
down the hill, something's rotting there.*

We don't live that far out in the country—
a smell still travels downwind; also
the sound of sawing, and harsh words
will get them refocusing their telescope

on our front windows. Lucky for us,
we'd thought, to find this place so thickly wooded;
Natural privacy, you'd called it.
Then came winter and the leaves fell away:

All the pets were happy, the dogs
in their baskets under the stairs,
the cats in their houses outside,
one on the front porch, one in back.

The baby was glad to watch all day
the cats mewing and rubbing the deck rails,
the dogs angling for snacks beneath the highchair,
and you and I content to watch him raspberry.

And when Minnie, the back door cat, went
missing, we told each other it was her yearly gadabout.
No, you said it was adventure; I'd seen
the matting of her coat, her antipathy to kibble.

It was no surprise then, Wednesday,
when you said, *I found Minnie, dead,*
and a cloud of her stink
blew in through the door.

So this is the dance the neighbors will see—
me with the shovel digging all day,
then you in your gas mask, mercifully
placing my flattened cat in her grave.

Wanted

to rewind when her friend's baby died
and the cat disappeared and then
her father's cancer came back. To pause

and rewind like a home-movie maker,
perfectly low-tech, on her personal Super-8.
She would not even worry about light—

back light or sunlight or the tungsten from the fixtures
in the examining room like the one where she'd
watched someone else's colonoscopy

on the video monitor while she waited for hers.
"His intestine was beautiful," she said afterwards,
"Clean and pearlescent, like a penis

turned inside out." The Versed was still working—
over and over she repeated the simile,
and the nurse just nodded. Wanted

to pause (as the doctor's scope had, at the other
guy's caecum—the moment she knew *he*
was fine) on the eve of her father's last CAT scan,

and splice it to a new today when his liver
and lungs would be clean... For what is art
but another kind of surgery? Ah,

but he'd refused the colostomy, claiming
quality of life. And now the film
was nearly over, and this time she wouldn't

just be undergoing a routine procedure,
but watching her father fade off screen.

Cancer in Manhattan

The day they found her husband's cancer
  it began to rain.
It was spring rain—warm and soaking
  and a whole week long.
And when it ended, the streets
  were new again, the pavement glittered,
the trees in their cages leafed out.

Not so her husband. No question
  but they'd try the chemo—
a slow drip weekly
  as spring would grow into summer
and the uptown streets empty
  of their wealthy residents.

On their walk up Lexington, that first Tuesday,
  a triplet of boys in blue uniforms passed them
at a run. *That could've been our sons,*
  remember how they came this way,
always running, always late? She reminisced
  as he huffed on, his coat unbuttoned.

She left him in the waiting room,
  Smithsonian in his hand,
the first week and the second,
  and went about her errands,
her standing appointment at the hairdresser,
  an hour beneath the helmet dryer,
Town and Country open on her lap.

The third week, he said *stay,*
  the magazines are all the same—
endangered auks, ads for Prozac.

I'd rather talk. What could she say?
Fifty-one years... It wasn't so long
ago she'd told her daughter
how he'd changed her life, took her
from wallflower to someone outgoing.
Here he was looking at her, but her tongue
was still. Should they go back to then,
the big picture—already—or just fill the time?
Foremost among her thoughts her mother's
mottoes: *put a good face on it; wish it away;
grin and bear it,* but cancer, Cancer!
Not even her father—a doctor—had beaten it.

That was digression. Why couldn't she face it,
face him? And again, digressing: above
his bed a picture: Van Gogh's *Wheat Fields with Reaper,*
a man in denim—her husband, she imagined,
before he'd come to college, or in summers in between—
that her family'd scorned. Why
should it have mattered he was poor?
Now she knows, but she stays dumb,
silent in the room of beeps and blips.

Just so, a whole year passed—
one after another poison cocktail
dripped into his veins. One turned him yellow,
another swelled him like a red balloon,
and still the cancer went on growing:
A nasty weed, he said he lay awake imagining,
choking all his organs. *Oh for a Garden Weasel™
to whack it back*—something from the back pages
of a magazine that would work miracles.

In the end, she was beside him,
    her eyes glazed, gazing at the painting above him,
which he must have seen upside down:
    An egg yolk in a yellow sea, toward which
a blue man dives, head first. Could
    departure be so easy? She looked at him
freshly now, his blue eyes sunken forever
    beneath the folds of flesh that were his lids,
and wanted to speak.

Seven

Christmas at Home

To my daughter, Helen

All the time that you were finishing up,
my dad was dying: 18 months of chemo
and still his cancer bore its fruit.
Meantime, in my womb, you rolled and squirmed
and swelled me like a Central Park balloon.
But I couldn't float away—the earthly
dying of my father bound me tight.

Then one night I dreamt that as I slept
my father held me, firmly, in his muscled arms.
I was tiny and could not wriggle loose...
or would not—his chest was gently heaving
and, like a newborn still learning how to breathe,
I cued on it and filled my lungs with air.

My father missed your slow arrival,
but now, untied, let's you and I fly on, together.

White-out

"Why does darkness make us not see?" — Paul

Once, in a snowstorm—the flakes falling sideways—
the car seemed to skate through tinny space while
the baby snored, my son asked Why? Why? Why?
and I, driving nearly blind, couldn't help but rest.

Why, Why, Why not close my eyes? I was crawling
down the two-lane county road, but there was no ice,
or deer on the shoulder in that snow, and no answer
why cold chills, snow flies, night comes, brights fail.

I might as well sleep, I told myself; I know
this road like the back of the baby's hand,
and something in sleep is equally delicate,
digits as fine as deer limbs in the distance.

Deer! My son need only know our eyes require
light's reflection, and I'll deny fatigue's opacity—
the stormy nights when high beams only hide the road
and instinct, simply, brings us bumping home.

Early Weaning

April should be a painting by a girl
who's just discovered green and green and green.
Yet when the new leaves suddenly unfurl—
tiny baby hands—the wrens seem still as sticks
and the mockingbirds don't sing their morning songs.

In the kitchen while I cut out biscuits
my infant daughter crawls commando-style.
Her goal's a chair leg or some Tupperware,
and once I find her eating afternoon—my watch so long
unused it's still on last year's daylight savings time.

Hunger draws us to each other—I feed
on feeding her and, once again, the milk
flowing and the birds outside unsilent,
I think of how I should—but won't—begin
to scrape my own encrusted palette clean.

July Fourth, 2003

Last Independence Day we bit the bullet,
brought our son to see my father—five screaming
hours North to where his makeshift farm
drained the family coffers one last year.
And at the little town's parade, Paul in overalls
rode his grandpa's shoulders, their two round faces
like moons come out too soon, moving to
the high school band's ba-boom ba-boom.

This Fourth, my father's gone and I leave early:
tack up before the heat has peaked, and ride
down a trail of blackberries, dreaming
of the day my son will want to come along,
knowing, though, he won't before the berries darken
and drop down and the trail has overgrown.

Christmas at Home

With a chainsaw, my girlfriend is Evel Knievel.
All day she rides it over the sourwoods
until they crack down in droves.
When she removes her orange helmet,
her gray hair spikes up into flames
and she tastes success's wisp of smoke.
She scans the land beyond the driveway;
the river birch shudders, "Don't cut me!"
and the spindly dogwoods of compulsion steel themselves.
Que sera sera!
George Washington threw a coin across the Delaware
to see if he could ford it, but she won't
dare the ailing hundred-year-old maple:
It will become a residence for woodpeckers
and come down branch by branch in summer thunderstorms
and dent the Sable and the Odyssey.
"Just so long as it doesn't hit the nursery...."
I used to be the butch one, but now
she lifts whole oaks and splits them at one blow
and soon the firewood reclines
in hungry piles among the underbrush.
This evening, though, her hands smell of sap
and the chainsaw is speechless.
No wonder—the firs are tied up in lights
and the front door creaks under garlands and wreaths.
This year we won't brave the river or cross the woods.

/

Andrea Selch has an MFA from UNC-Greensboro, and a PhD from Duke University, where she taught creative writing from 1999 until 2003. Her poems have appeared in *Calyx, Equinox, The Greensboro Review, Oyster Boy Review, Luna, The MacGuffin,* and *Prairie Schooner.* Her first chapbook, *Succory,* was published by Carolina Wren Press in 2000. *Startling* was originally published by Turning Point Press in 2004, after placing in the 2003 Turning Point competition, and has been reissued here by Cockeyed Press. Her second chapbook, *Boy Returning Water to the Sea: Koans for Kelly Fearing,* was also published in 2009 by Cockeyed Press. In 2001, she joined the board of Carolina Wren Press and is now its President and Executive Director. She lives in rural Hillsborough, North Carolina, with her partner and their two children. For information about upcoming readings, please visit www.andreaselch.com.

Printed in the USA
CPSIA information can be obtained
at www.ICGtesting.com
JSHW012045140824
68134JS00034B/3273